# Heart Matters

## A Poetic Revolution of Truth, Healing, and Belonging

Shahmeen Aruna Sadiq

Heart Matters

A Poetic Revolution of Truth, Healing, and Belonging

Poetry, essays and illustrations by Shahmeen Aruna Sadiq



Published by Brave Healer Productions

# DEDICATION

This book is for the children.

For Jordan and Lukas:

You are the lights of my life. I've made choices along the way that were difficult. Please know that every one of them was for the highest good and best outcome for you. Words cannot describe the depth and breadth of my love for you.

For Sara:

I feel so lucky that life brought us to each other.

For all the children:

May you always know you are not alone.

*"Shahmeen has written a book of thoughts and feelings, essays and poems, filled with grace, the hope within heartbreak, and the deeply personal yet universal passages to becoming. This is a soul journey here, and the reflective contemplative writing here speaks to generative, and generational healing. May you find yourself in these offerings, and see the grace of falling in love with your own heart."*

~ **Chris Wahl**, President, Miro Group Consulting LLC,
Founder and Creator of the Leadership Coaching program
at Georgetown University and Co-author of *Be Your Own Coach*
with Barbara Braham, and *On Becoming a Leadership Coach*
with Clarice Scriber, and Beth Bloomfield.

---

*"From the first time I met Shahmeen, it was clear that she is a fierce pioneer of the inner world. She is unflinching in her commitment to her own growth and that of others. This book is a rare window into a courageous story and a beautiful soul. May it support you on your journey to your own truth and healing."*

~ **Bob Anderson**, Creator of The Leadership Circle™
and Co-author of *Mastering Leadership*
and *Scaling Leadership* with William Adams

---

*"In these pages you will find an authentic voice describing what it takes to heal and grow into a happy, compassionate and loving human being. You will undoubtedly recognize some aspect of your own journey in the poems and prose pieces that Shahmeen offers. Prepare to be touched, moved, inspired and encouraged as you engage with Heart Matters."*

~ **Barbara Braham**, Ph.D., MCC. Author of *Finding Your Purpose*

---

*"Shahmeen, through her rich and poignant writing, guides us beautifully through the arc of the wound. From woundedness, she uses curiosity to seek out, discover, and share her unique, divine purpose to not only bring more joy to herself but to make the world a better place. And the world is a better place because of her and this beautiful book. You will see yourself reflected in her words and can use them to find your way to your divine purpose."*

~ **Tomi Llama**, Author of *What's Your Superpower?*, *The Tomi Llama Divine Purpose Guide*, and *Hating Myself Every Step Of The Way*

---

*"When it comes to matters of the heart, there is no one I trust more than Shahmeen Sadiq. In this book she shares years of time tested, heartfelt, nuggets of wisdom that have been born out of her own direct experience. Each poem offers a glimpse into her personal journey through many layers of circumstantial challenges, intense inner work, ever present refining, and immense growth. Between the covers of this priceless treasure chest of poetry, Shahmeen shares the twists, turns, ups, downs, and profound insights that life has invited her to notice and embody. Immerse yourself in this wisdom and let it support you in the transformation of your big, bright, beautiful heart. If you do, I sense you will find that Your Heart matters!"*

~ **Jim Anderson**, President, Key-Connections, Inc. and Author of *How To Find a Silver Lining In Every Dark Cloud*

---

# FOREWORD

Have you ever been introduced to someone for the very first time, and with your initial few shared words felt in your bones that you recognized them, had known them all your life?

Thirty years ago, when the man I was dating (now my husband) introduced me to his daughter Shahmeen, that was precisely my experience. We quickly found we were asking the same questions, completing one another's sentences, challenging assumptions using the same words. It was uncanny!

Shahmeen was 21 years old at the time, two and a half years older than my eldest daughter. And, like most 21-year-olds, she was vibrating with the youthful energy of endless curiosity and life's magnificent possibilities. Just a short couple of years after that first meeting, Shahmeen courageously made real one of those life possibilities, leaving her home, friends, and work in Ottawa to move in with her father and me in Toronto and continue her university education.

Back then, I was impressed by Shahmeen's obvious clarity of purpose, courage, and love of learning; qualities she still embodies today. And—like all of us beautifully imperfect human beings—there were times she wasn't as clear as she could be, second-guessed herself, and doubted that she was enough. The wonder for me was that even at that young age, Shahmeen didn't allow those thoughts to spin round and round inside for very long, gaining more power and control with each cycle. She trusted herself enough to be open and vulnerable, to speak aloud what she was experiencing, and even to be curious about it. And she trusted me enough to ask for my listening ear.

Providing a listening ear comes naturally to me. As a child of a mentally ill parent, I grew up watching and listening for signs that a breakdown was on the horizon. Through an often painful three-year therapy process, as well as numerous personal growth workshops over the years, I learned to trust my intuition and listen to the wisdom in my body and the love in my heart.

Professionally, during my training and work globally as an organization development consultant, certified psychotherapist, and leadership development coach, I've learned to meet individuals where they are; to listen for the emotions often hidden deep beneath body language and words designed to maintain an "I'm in control, all is right" protective mask.

And, in fact, all is right—even when we're feeling out of control, lost, confused, or fearful. I say that because I have long believed that each of us is here to fulfill a unique purpose, and the situations, experiences, and interactions life sends our way are designed precisely to help us learn and grow, revealing the Beings we're meant to be in order to live that purpose. I am forever grateful that over the years Shahmeen has shared with me the details of the many situations, experiences, and interactions sent to help her learn and grow. And what she may not fully appreciate is the degree to which accompanying her on that thirty-year unfolding of all she's meant to be in this world has helped me learn and grow, as well.

As I write these words, I'm thinking especially about Shahmeen's incredible commitment to her personal development. She is, for example, beautifully able to hold another with respect and positive regard, even in the midst of highly emotional disagreements. She welcomes even deeply uncomfortable feelings, and then asks herself what her own contribution was to the situation, and what she can learn moving forward. She is a role model for me in this.

As a mother, Shahmeen is very aware that her behaviour is setting an example, not of perfection, but of honesty, self-confidence, vulnerability, humour, and humanity. It's a delight for me to see how my teenaged grandchildren are learning from her.

Shahmeen has become an exceptional coach, working with organizational leaders and other coaches to support them in their learning and development. And because of her own deep personal work, she brings to every interaction a fierce belief in the good within her clients' hearts and a caring compassion for the often-painful challenges of their journey. It's not easy working with Shahmeen—it's life changing.

And then there's her writing. I can't help but laugh when I remember sitting with Shahmeen's father during those back-to-university years, scouring her essays clean of grammatical errors.

Magically, as she learned increasingly to trust herself and to listen to the wisdom in her own heart, Shahmeen's written words have become poetry. Powerful poetry. As I read Shahmeen's work, my own life's pain, wonder, fear, and grief echo in my heart. As I read her words, I feel that I am her. She is me. I am her mother. And she is mine.

It's no coincidence that Shahmeen became a part of my life, and no coincidence that I became a part of hers; the wisdom of the universe in action! It's also no coincidence that Shahmeen is releasing her book of deeply insightful, emotionally raw poetry right now, as our world struggles to heal itself from the ravages of COVID, hundreds of years of racial and economic injustice, and ongoing denial of the climate crisis we human beings have caused. Each one of us who aches with the pain of loss, suffers in silence with shame, longs to be seen and heard, yearns to love and be loved, needs to read Shahmeen's poetry. And our world needs us to read this poetry with eyes and hearts wide open.

I'm excited for you to breathe in every word.

Linda Mitz Sadiq

Toronto, Canada

May 13, 2021

S. Sadiq
April 2019

# TO MY BELOVED READERS

I've felt invisible for pretty much my entire life.

As a little girl of colour growing up in the 1970s, when Toronto was not the diverse and bustling city it is today, I recall only too clearly the physical and emotional attacks leveled at me and my younger brother. It was bewildering. What had we done to deserve this? Why were we being singled out in this way? And where were the adults who were supposed to protect us? I recall schoolyard beatings, horrible slurs, harrowing chases; me on foot, them on bikes. You might think, *wow, she was anything BUT invisible to attract that kind of ferocity.* You're right. On the outside, it was clear that our strange lunches and brown skin were different. But on the inside, I always felt the real "me" was neither seen nor respected. I was inhuman to them—an object to kick around; a plaything. That's what I mean by invisible; my humanity was not acknowledged and I did not exist in their eyes.

Perhaps you can resonate with this experience. One doesn't need dark skin to know this feeling.

To survive, I had to do three things: First, become capable, because I could not rely on anyone else to help me. Second, become nice, friendly, and agreeable, so I could love them into not harming me. Third, become smart so the adults in my life would accept me and therefore not be able to abandon me.

These coping strategies helped me build character, and I consider them gifts—even though they were born out of a fear of annihilation that no child should ever experience. I've since learned that many people have grown up in similarly terrifying circumstances. More than you'd ever believe.

As the years unfolded, I suppose I got used to feeling that I didn't belong or matter; that I wasn't enough and would never be validated by the outside world. And there was some force of grace that traveled along beside those doubts that prompted me to keep going, nonetheless. I accumulated experiences, skills, and qualities and became less and less afraid to grab ahold of opportunities that interested me. My gifts of willpower (capability), heart (niceness), and intellect (smartness) supported me to reach for more ways to achieve, serve, and create. I began to tune into the extraordinary preciousness of life and, as I grew through motherhood, a strong vow emerged that my life should be put into service of great things that help human beings in grounded, practical, and tangible ways.

Today I'm the owner of my own human and leadership development consultancy. I've traveled across the globe and have friends in numerous countries. I am known as a loving facilitator who speaks to the depth of human experience. I'm a trusted adviser to leaders and organizations, and I have taught and mentored hundreds of professionals to work in this deeper way.

I've woven my potent offering together out of colourful, eclectic, and diverse strands: meditation, nutrition, ancestral healing, energy work, leadership development, accessing guidance and intuition, skydiving, dancing, art, poetry, and more. The resultant tapestry is extraordinarily rich and I feel blessed to have touched so many of you with my heartfelt invitation to be seen, heard, and respected so that you, too, can make a significant contribution with your own life and work.

The poems and memoirs in the following pages chronicle aspects of my life's journey and may mirror or resonate with yours. I share hard topics in this book; I'm known for being fierce and compassionate and utterly honest—all at the same time. I believe in speaking about what is going on, how I feel, and what I'm noticing. And I'm passionate about inviting you to do the same. No more whitewashing, projecting, or tiptoeing around things.

I dream of a world where humans accept each other and connect in these deeper places to find our shared experience and begin to regard and respect each other as fellow humans who yearn for the same things: to be seen, to be heard, to live life fully, to experience love, to know we matter simply because we exist.

If you've ever felt invisible, and you recognize yourself through these pages, please know that my heart is with the beautifully woven tapestry that is you!

Shahmeen Sadiq

Toronto, Canada

May 2021

# TABLE OF CONTENTS

**FOREWORD** ........ **viii**

**TO MY BELOVED READERS** ........ **xiii**

**AWAKENING** ........ **1**

Awakening ........ 3

She Who Hears the Cries of the World ........ 5

The Agony of Awareness ........ 8

The Blessing ........ 9

Does God Weep? ........ 11

Declaration ........ 13

Vision Trees ........ 15

Tangle of Emotions ........ 16

Impermanent Roles ........ 18

Haunted ........ 20

A Hug ........ 22

**REFLECTING** ........ **24**

Reflecting ........ 26

You Shouldn't Talk ........ 28

Ode to a Lost Childhood ........ 30

I Wish ........ 37

Who Am I and Why Am I Here? ........ 38

Who Am I Becoming? .......... 40
Sorting Through Old Clothes .......... 42
Enough .......... 43
**MAKING FRIENDS WITH MYSELF .......... 44**
Making Friends With Myself .......... 46
Grace's Circle .......... 48
It's Possible That I'm The Asshole .......... 51
The Truth and The Way .......... 53
Don't Turn Away .......... 54
Surrender .......... 55
Transformation .......... 56
**YEARNING TO MATTER .......... 57**
Yearning to Matter .......... 58
Unjust Desserts .......... 60
The Path of the Other .......... 65
Enchained .......... 66
Zero Some .......... 67
Willing Rage .......... 70
The Invisible Woman .......... 74
**LOVING .......... 76**
Loving .......... 78
What I Want You to Know .......... 80
Infatuation .......... 83
Infatuation II .......... 84
Ambitious Healing .......... 85
Why? .......... 86
A Challenge to Love .......... 87
Healing Relationship Prayer .......... 88
Let's Say .......... 89

Acceptance ........ 90
Don't Fall In Love With Your Theories ........ 91

**SACRED EXCHANGES ........ 93**

Sacred Exchanges ........ 94
Our Human Family ........ 96
Enter the Sacred ........ 98
Joy Endures ........ 99
Another Beginning ........ 100
Music Got Dropped ........ 102
Weary Warrior ........ 104
What Would the Earth Say, If She Could Speak Through Me? ..... 105
Do It Now ........ 107
Mantra for Difficult Days ........ 109
Return to Dance ........ 110
Enough's Invitation ........ 111
The Dawn of The Fierce Love ........ 112
Unity ........ 113

**MY INVITATION TO YOU ........ 114**

**ACKNOWLEDGEMENTS ........ 117**

**ABOUT THE AUTHOR ........ 120**

# Awakening

"Donal's Invitation"

# AWAKENING

*Have you ever felt the Wave of Insistence? It's the flow and the force that does NOT force, but that quietly, gently, and sometimes fiercely insists that you be who you really are.*

*You are aware, no doubt, of other forces in your life that have told you who you're supposed to be, how you're supposed to be, and what you're supposed to do.*

*I was born into a culture where doctors are highly revered and respected as the source and fountain of the truth. As early as I can remember, adults in my life told me repeatedly that I was destined to occupy the medical profession. Since this was so strongly ingrained in me, I never considered any other possibility for my life.*

*I dug into my schoolwork and refused to study anything beyond the compulsory courses and every science and math course available. With focus and speed, I completed five years of high school in four. I raced towards I don't know what, but certainly ran furiously away from my heart. Overachiever that I was, I headed into engineering, reasoning that it would be even better to start this way before adding medical school later. I had it all planned out.*

*However, it turned out that I hated everything about engineering. I failed with unthinkably low marks after my first semester, and an academic adviser shared stern words with me: "Miss Sadiq, it appears that engineering is not for you. My advice is to leave now, before you get kicked out. Then you can return next year, but please choose a different course of study."*

*At the tender age of 18, I was completely lost.*

*The Wave of Insistence does not insist that we be something that we are not, rather it insists that we become who we really are.*

*The following poems and pieces were written at a time when the Wave of Insistence was finally getting my attention. It was a seriously disruptive time, but absolutely essential for me to become all I really am and to do all that I am here to do. Though I was led through very difficult situations, I remain grateful every day that I was able to awaken to its call.*

# SHE WHO HEARS THE CRIES OF THE WORLD

I hear the cries all the time.

It's impossible to shut them out. The incessant wailing of a hungry baby at the airport that pierces my heart and brings me to tears every time. The brown, sandy surface of the mountains in Utah begging us to stop sucking the planet dry. The unspoken longing of the child inside another who just wants to be seen, held, and loved. Early in the game I said yes to building my life around a response to these cries. "Do something," is the essence of their song. "Mommy, do something!" And Mommy does.

I've been learning about Guan Yin (also known as Kwan Yin), the Goddess of Mercy and Compassion. It seems I embody a great number of her qualities: compassion, caring, listening and hearing, a special affinity for children, as well as the ability to see inside another and aid in the healing of illusions[1]. The more I read about Guan Yin, the more resonance I feel in my heart. My sense of her, and of myself, is that of a *great mother* who has come to work in support of *the* Great Mother: Mother Earth.

It's a gift; a wonderful, powerful gift I have been given. Would it be fair to say that I've chosen to cultivate it? No. It is more accurate to say that it chose me and I was compelled to cooperate. People say that the most profound things happen when they receive this gift. It is wonderful to know I'm on purpose. When the conversations are coming to a close I feel expanded, joyous, energized, alive. A win-win for all, in that moment. The good feeling can last up to a few hours. The income I have earned in doing this has allowed me to create a home and life for myself and my boys—a wondrous feat as a single mother—something I'm so grateful for.

1 http://www.sacredwind.com/kuanyin.php

One Buddhist legend says that the goddess Guan Yin vowed never to rest until she freed all beings from samsara, or reincarnation. "Despite strenuous effort, she realized that still many unhappy beings were yet to be saved. After struggling to comprehend the needs of so many, her head split into eleven pieces. Amitabha Buddha, seeing her plight, gave her eleven heads with which to hear the cries of the suffering. Upon hearing these cries and comprehending them, Guan Yin attempted to reach out to all those who needed aid, but found that her two arms shattered into pieces. Once more, Amitabha came to her aid and appointed her a thousand arms with which to aid the many."[2]

It's a terrible burden, this gift I've been given. My twenty-two fascinated, tired eyes see the emails coming in, while a slow bilious terror begins to burn inside my chest. My head feels like it will explode as I try to keep up with the onslaught of demand. I fear I will be consumed, and may even cease to exist if this continues! I'm overwhelmed with their need, their grasping, their longing for me. In my peri-menopausal state it feels like I've been tasked with holding the very planet in my slippery womb all day without letting it fall, where it would surely shatter and soak through the professional projection I've managed to maintain. It hurts, this gift.

It's not a comfortable conversation to have with any of my peers: "Oh, I've created this profitable business out of doing what I love and offering my gifts and people are asking for it all over the place and by the way, I'm thinking of packing it in because I'm so tired, so very fucking tired." Most of them would kill for what they think I have. I see the envious longing in their eyes after I've complained about my perceived success, and sigh and begin all over again. How shameful of me to make them feel small. I shouldn't complain, I should be grateful. I must make them feel better.

I yearn for a reprieve from the low level of worry that accompanies this gift. If we are to make up for hurting another by caring for three, then I wonder what heinous crimes I have committed in a past life that resulted in this need to care for the entire human race?

Guan Yin offers me another possibility. Rather than seek to grow an extra nine hundred and ninety-eight arms to meet the demand, it may be time to turn her/my gifts towards myself. Perhaps I have mistaken the remedy *in here* for a purpose *out there!* Maybe the only people I need to care for this time are my own inner children; my own parched landscape. Simple

2 http://www.nationsonline.org/oneworld/Chinese_Customs/Guan_Yin.htm

basic needs are what get compromised when I succumb to the grandiose illusions that *I am* the mother of the world, that it is all up to *me*, that I'm *the only one,* and that *I must do it all myself.* Maybe that is the great joke here. Maybe that is the gift.

# THE AGONY OF AWARENESS

*The Undulation of Life describes the flow between expansive and contracting experiences. Group retreats that focus on personal development of all kinds are normally expanding. As the group gels and the exploration deepens, a heightened sense of potency and empowerment overtakes the group: expansion. In the hours or days following such an experience, participants may feel a crushing low: contraction. This can feel terrifying. Sometimes I've wondered if I would literally die, because the difference between the high of expansion and the low of contraction is so wide. We talk about this in my workshops so that people will know what to expect if/when the contraction comes. If this happens to you, please be extra kind to yourself and know it's a normal and temporary state.*

*This poem, one of my first, was written while in the midst of the contraction after a life-changing week as a participant in a leadership development workshop in 2008.*

Here in the dance of my everyday life
I find my thoughts drifting back to yesterday.

Images, feelings, sensations torment my body and squeeze my heart
Memories of those delicious moments of connection
The thrill of being awake: witnessed and witnessing
The sensual intertwining of souls
How I long for this depth of love, always!

I try to distract myself, knowing this yearning will soon fade into the background
and there will be other times for us
Yet that is little comfort today.

# THE BLESSING

I pulled into my driveway, thinking about what was next in my calendar for the afternoon. As I gathered my stuff from the passenger seat, I noticed an elderly man making his way gingerly along the sidewalk towards me. I saw this man with the weathered brown face many times in the years since we moved to this home. Every time we acknowledged each other with a smile, a nod, and a quiet "hello". But this time was different.

Something compelled me to time my exit from the vehicle with his arrival in front of my house. The word *blessing* came to mind as I watched him painstakingly placing his foot down with each excruciatingly slow step. I said hello and walked towards him in the brilliant sunshine of the crisp fall day.

He stopped and began speaking to me. "My knees are paining me," he said with a grimace.

"Oh dear," I said sympathetically, "Is it the cold that causes them to hurt?"

"No, they always ache," he said.

"I can see that they hurt when you are walking," I said.

"Yes, it is quite painful."

"Do you live close by?"

"Yes," and he gave his address.

I held out my hand and introduced myself, "My name is Shahmeen."

He took my hand and grasped it tightly, then raised it to his lips and kissed it. "God bless you," he said, as the wrinkles deepened around his shining eyes.

"God bless YOU," I mumbled, amazed at the fact that he was vocalizing my earlier thoughts.

In that moment, it was as if an energy field had settled around us, and although I don't consider myself a religious person, I can say that I felt the presence of God with his touch. We dropped hands and locked eyes. Then he took my hand again and held it in both of his. I can't recall what he said, and what he said really didn't matter. It was the depth of connection between us that was profound and spoke volumes that didn't need to be given words in order to be understood. We shared something of the love, depth, and unity that exists between humans; a true gift of this moment.

He continued on his way and I went inside to resume my day. *I AM blessed,* I thought. I am blessed to have the family I have, to have the colleagues I have, and to be engaged in bringing forth this work of my heart.

# DOES GOD WEEP?

*During a tumultuous time of personal transformation, whenever I heard or read about violence, I received a vision of a similar scenario playing out. Except the vision always included one of my own children as the victim.*

*On the day this guidance came through, instead of trying to move away from the feelings the experience evoked, I allowed myself to stay with them. I intentionally breathed the sorrow and fear, deeply and fully, into each cell of my body. Although the emotional pain was immense, I felt healing take place when choosing to surrender rather than engaging in my usual resistance.*

*As I lay weeping, I wondered whether God sheds tears over the violence we perpetrate against each other. Moments later I received the following words:*

My children, I weep
when I see you forgetting
who you are.

You are brothers and sisters.
The divine spirit shines brightly upon
and within you.
Alas, you cannot see it when you are
blinded by fear and confusion.

When you murder, you are killing us all.
You have forgotten our birthright
which is to live with joy, love and happiness.

The time is now, so hasten to tear
off the masks which blind you
to the joining that is longed for.

My children, I weep.

# DECLARATION

I am worthy of receiving love and celebration for all of who I am. I no longer need to be wounded, tragic, dramatic, or sick in order to feel worthy of love.

I can feel and express love for another person without having to find their wounds. I can love them just because I do.

*The next five poems are the first poems I ever wrote as an adult. One Christmas, my family gathered at a retreat my parents built in the country. My marriage was crumbling. My partner and I had the usual pressures young families feel: kids, careers, money, house, etc. But the real issue was that I was beginning to feel the dissonance that answering the call of my own heart evoked.*

*You see, our wounds brought us together in the first place. I needed someone to tell me what to do, and he had such a powerful presence when we met. A perfect fit, right? Except that now I was beginning to hear and heed the invitation that the Wave of Insistence offered—to step into my own power—and this meant I was changing the deal we unconsciously made when we came together.*

*I knew it had to come to a close, but with two young children and all the guilt the thought of leaving him raised, I knew the process would be slow. I tolerated it well, but sometimes rage-filled impatience would overwhelm me. That day, I felt guided to put on my boots, grab my camera, and announce that I was going for a walk—alone.*

*The trees beckoned me forward from my state of utter frustration into an extraordinary experience of grace. Each one I was invited to photograph spoke a poem. Somehow I was able to retain the poems long enough to write them down after returning to the house. Because the photos were taken with less-than optimal resolution, I've created charcoal renderings of some of them so I can share them with you.*

# VISION TREES

What do I want?

So many outcomes

It is important not to be too
attached to the path or even to what
it will look like when I get there

Hold the vision

Listen for guidance from the wind:

*stop racing*

*stand still*

*receive*

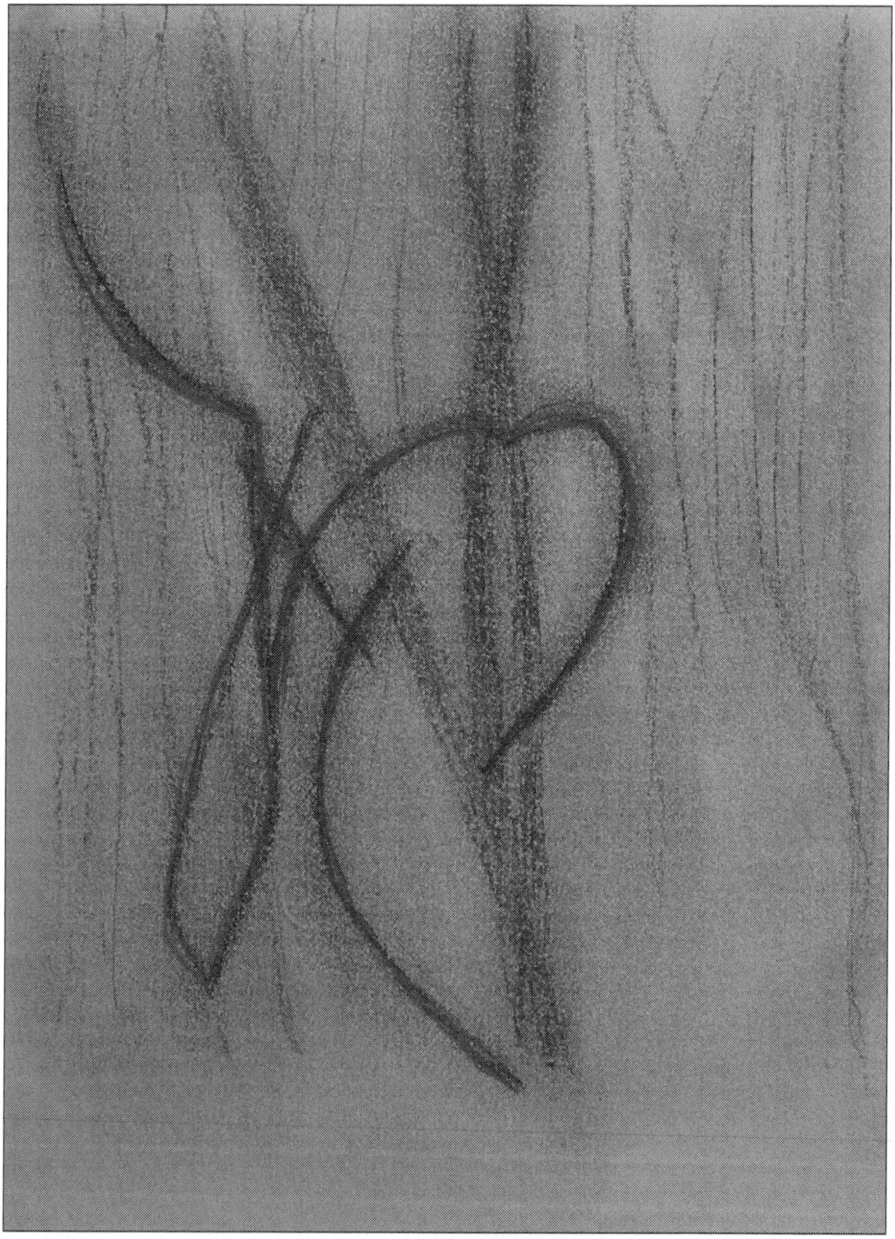

# TANGLE OF EMOTIONS

Confused.

Exhausted by the tangled
emotions in my heart,

I try to breathe in space so
that clarity can be found.

Then I realize that clarity and
order are illusions.

Look at the beauty of this
messiness!

It is worthy of love.

# IMPERMANENT ROLES

although neither stands straight and solid,
we are here to lean into and be leaned upon

today I relax into your embrace
tomorrow you ask for my counsel

both loving that we
have found each other

# HAUNTED

How I continue to live
with so much darkness in my soul
amazes me

I can love you, then hate you,
both with perfect passion

I want to nurture, be protected,
then I push you away
longing to be left by myself

Haunted by variations of these questions:
Am I alone?
Are we connected?
Who are we?
What did I agree to when I embarked on this journey?

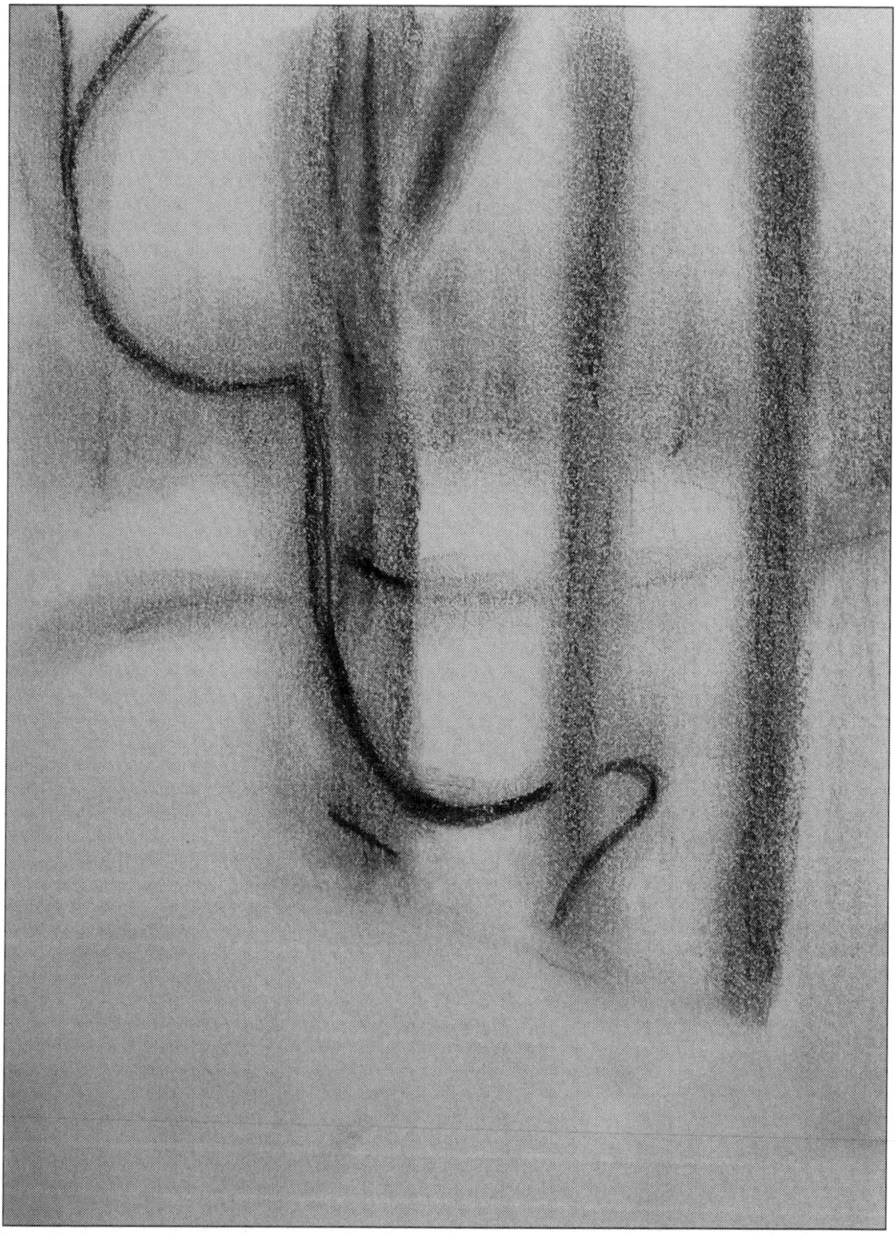

# A HUG

After the torment, there is some relief
I wrap my arms around myself in a warm hug
Reminded, once again, that soothing is available here
How I love myself! You! Us! This!
Grateful
There is always an abundance of love
I only need to know this

# Reflecting

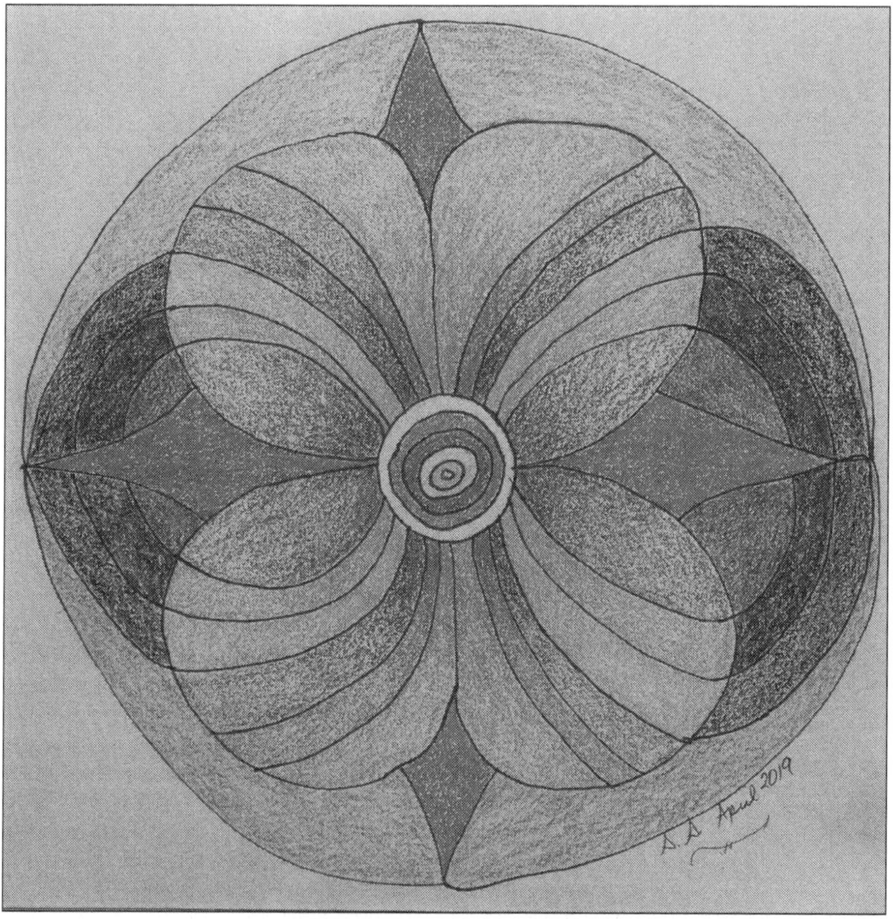
April 2019

# REFLECTING

*As I write these introductions to each group of poems, I am well into the fifty-first year of this human experience I am so blessed to live. Thanks to the privilege of so much time passing, I can more easily see patterns, themes, and threads that were previously hidden from my view. It's fascinating to look back and observe the shape of my journey to where I am today.*

# YOU SHOULDN'T TALK

The door of the small bathroom always creaked when it opened, but I learned to move it ever so slowly, a little at a time, while pulling down on the smooth, round doorknob just enough with both hands so I could listen to the grown-ups in the living room across the hall before being seen. My mother was on the phone in the kitchen that day, which was around the corner and up one step, so for sure she couldn't see me.

On this summer evening in August, I stood looking down at my skinny legs streaked with dirt from a hot summer day spent in the park with our housekeeper-who-was-also-a-nanny, Marjorie. I was the kind of child who soaked up a lot from the people around me, especially the adults. So naturally I tuned into my mom's conversation and heard the bit about Claire's mom. As I drift back to that time in my mind's eye, it's hard to recall exactly what was said. Was it that she was pretentious or overprotective? I cannot recall the precise words, but was astute enough to glean that whatever it was, it was not something to aspire to.

The years from grades one through four were a roller coaster ride for me with Claire; swinging between the extremes of love and hate, friendship and enmity, inclusion and exclusion. It was on one of the "out" days when I hurled the thing I had overheard about her mother at her, undoubtedly with an intention to cause pain. The backlash was immediate, hot, and stingingly injurious. "Well, you don't even HAVE a mother, so you shouldn't talk!"

After breaking down in uncontrollable tears, sobbing through Claire's and the witnesses' explanations to the teacher of what had unfolded, and spending some time alone in the nurse's office so I could calm down, her comment shut me up indeed. I turned inward. *I have a mother. Of course I do! What is she talking about? Why would she say that?*

My parents were in the groundless dance of marital breakup by then, and it was anyone's guess which one would be at home when we returned from school each day. I suppose that by this time in my life, I was so used to the unsettledness of my life that it had become normal for me, so this statement about my lack of a mother was jarring and felt so unfair. Just because she wasn't there all the time didn't mean she didn't exist!

Today I was browsing my social media feeds and I saw some powerful videos of famous black men sharing: *When I first realized I was black.* The incident with Claire marks the moment: *When I first realized I was different.* Growing up in the elite and gossipy Leaside area of Toronto in the early 1970's, the norm was very much the *Leave It to Beaver*-type families. You know, the wholesome, white, supportive households led by a working father and a stay-at-home, June Cleaver-like mother. To be a member of a brown-skinned family led by two professional, working parents made one stand out for sure. Then to have those parents be in the process of divorce; well, it became crystal clear that day that I was the ONLY one having THAT experience. It was the worst thing that could happen at that age.

Many things changed after that. I became keenly ashamed of myself: for provoking Claire's attack, and for having the nerve to comment on someone else's situation when mine was obviously no shining model of perfection. I turned from a happy, carefree little being into the shy, tentative, and fearful girl I have long since recognized, walking through my days cautiously, careful not to cause friction or look undone, even when things were falling apart all around me.

# ODE TO A LOST CHILDHOOD

running
jumping for joy
dusty legs
pebbles stuck
between my toes
wind-tousled hair
sun-kissed cheeks

this is the childhood that
was too quickly lost
in favour of grades and studying
and achievement and *setting*
*yourself up well for the future*

also the adults
who were
supposed to nurture us
were preoccupied with
grown-up things
so we learned
if we needed it
to get it ourselves

latch-key mini-chefs
a long welt on my left arm
from where the red-hot
element singed my flesh
as I lifted the tray of
dense lasagna I had prepared
out of the oven to serve
my siblings their dinner
I was only ten or eleven
years old at the time
But who's counting?

tender aged independence
don't do something for
a child that they can do
for themselves, they say
for some like me
it went too far
in reverse

I don't know which is more heartbreaking
The child who became a
grown-up far too early?
The grown-ups who
failed to notice her pain?

my four year old niece
knows already
to sit quietly and wait
while I check my phone
a stark difference
from my own teenage boys who
still remember what it was
like when I was present with them

they make loving, then sarcastic
comments about the
tech ban
that doesn't work

both ways
and when I finally
distractedly look up
...because I just need to finish THIS first...
they've already given up
and gone away

What's the point?
she's more interested in her email, Facebook,
LinkedIn, who is doing what out there
than anything we could need or offer

when I'm finally ready
I find them on the Xbox
or Snapchatting
zoned out
too busy for me now
an ironic consequence

I don't know which is more heartbreaking
The little girl who has
only known distraction?
My boys who remember
different times?

anger, separation, an endless
litany of guns, voluntarily
terrorizing ourselves over and
over again with our choices of
what to watch, what to consume
what goes viral, what becomes normal

I don't know which is more heartbreaking
My own fascination with what is wrong?
Our mutual acceptance of our unimportance?
The planet and our great human family
hurtling towards extinction?

my heartbreak leads me out
this morning
off the treadmill of habit
to a slow walk
on snow-dusted icy streets
treacherously healing
one foot carefully placed down
before committing my weight
to that leg
testing for slipperyness or grip
focused on reading the land
to find the surest path forward

memories of the innocent days
of skipping
jumping
running
and tumbling
trickle back in
around the edges of
my reverie
along with
sharp breaths
periodically punctuating
this song when I slide
never falling
on hidden ice
awakening me to my fragility
underneath all this competence

I followed the footprints
in the snow today
to my special spot
at the bluffs, thinking,
I'm not the only person
who is drawn to stand here
and gaze at the splendour
and peace and serenity

of the morning sun
to let the world of cars
and deadlines fade away
and hear the cheerful birdsong
of hope as spring dawns

I am older now
approaching the "half-time" as
one forty-something social media
superstar assures me
It's not too late, he shouts,
you have a whole other half of your life
to create what matters

I don't know what to do now
many mattering threads float
around me like wispy trails of smoke
from a wood-fired stove
(I smelled that on my return today
walking on Kingston Road
why does it smell like the country
on this busy street, I recall thinking)

I have been grieving
this lost childhood
since I was five years old
maybe longer
because I'm not really sure
at what age I began to care
for my little brother

who will take care of him
if I don't? I wondered
they're so busy yelling
they haven't noticed that
he doesn't know how to
put his shirt, socks and pants
on by himself
or use a spoon to eat his soup

without spilling it down
the front of his t-shirt

for many years all it
took was the sound of a
baby or small child crying
to set me off
fountains of tears
with no notice
even in public places

it's embarrassing
to cry so easily
and trying to stop it
is fruitless
then it comes out
a graceless explosion
from my nose
better to surrender
let the well of grief through

is it any wonder then
that all I want to do
now is play
make art
write poems
go outside
create films
host gatherings
coach basketball
cook delicious food
and eat it

Is this my second half?
A return to the careless, playful, freedom of childhood?

Could this be the remedy for me, for my children, for the planet?
All I know is useless now
guidance says it is time

to be free, dance joyously,
purposelessly
simply for the fun of it

I don't know which is more heartbreaking
A life of purpose set aside
in favour of play when
there is so much work
to be done?
The cost of denying
myself this healing
that this lost little girl
so desperately craves?

# I WISH

I wish that they could see
me suffering inside
I wish someone would say,
"Come child, rest your weary head."
I wish I could have told them
about the burden I was carrying
I wish to have not felt
so very alone

# WHO AM I AND WHY AM I HERE?

I am a mother, here to model what it is to truly take care of myself, so that my children will learn how to do the same.

I am a survivor, here to stay true to who I am and what I stand for, no matter the circumstances.

I am a partner, here to give and receive in service of our larger impact in the world.

I am a lover, here to love with joy and be joyfully loved.

I am the sun, here to warm the back of your neck as you gaze out over the ocean.

I am the snow, falling invisibly and coating mountain peaks with shimmering light.

I am a stone, whose shape and path is determined by the flowing water and the certainty of gravity.

I am a skydiver, here to leap gracefully even when faced with fear that can keep me rooted in place.

I am a builder of communities, here to bring us together so that we can more effectively and powerfully do our work in the world.

I am an insatiable little girl, who adores and is adored.

I am a woman, here to move with grace, dignity and purpose through my journey.

I am you, here to reflect and mirror presence.

I am the world, within my body and experience, lives all that brings sorrow and peace to humanity.

I am a spiritual warrior, here to hold what is seemingly opposite, yet remarkably, remaining still, grounded and connected to my Source.

I am a goddess, here to radiate with beauty, love and compassion.

# WHO AM I BECOMING?

I've heard myself ask these questions
over and over of myself and my clients:
Who are you?
Why are you here?
What is the gift or contribution you are here to offer?

The question of
*Who am I becoming?*
is quite different, and intriguing indeed.

A brain teaser of sorts.

Cause if we're not talking about
my accomplishments,
my talents,
what I have been known for,
who I serve
or how much money I make

then

how can I respond?

Who am I becoming?

Who I have always been:
Me
Enough
Worthy
Valuable
Lovable
Beautiful
Me.

Ah.

# SORTING THROUGH OLD CLOTHES

I put down this cloak of blame
I take off this coat of shame
I unwrap this shawl of helplessness
and put them all away

They served me well, way back then and yesterday
kept me safe and away from pain

Where I'm sitting now
I feel I don't need them anymore

In this moment of nakedness
I'm not sure what to do
So I'll sit here quietly, awaiting the new
Vestments that were woven long ago
And are already on their way

As they arrive I unpack and delight
Each piece will take time to fully become mine
And, that is all right.

# ENOUGH

I am enough, as I am
It is enough, as it is
Let me, and it, be enough
Enough love, work and friends
I am enough

# Making Friends With Myself

# MAKING FRIENDS WITH MYSELF

*These poems, though perhaps painful to read, shine light onto what I refer to as "that which is in shadow". What is in shadow is invisible to the human eye, and if you don't bring what is in shadow into the light, I believe you'll forever be at its mercy. Naming, seeing, and processing the less-than-optimal events of your younger years can be incredibly liberating, despite the pain. It can also be quite triggering, so please make sure you are well supported as you begin your process of inquiring into your shadow parts.*

# GRACE'S CIRCLE

I have felt over recent weeks that I am being honoured by opportunities to experience a state of grace. Many events, signs and signals are pointing me to a feeling of deep connection with the essential.

I awoke in the middle of the night last night with the following story about my relationship with my mother front and centre in my mind, demanding to be written. Reluctantly I got up and attempted to capture the essence of it on my computer:

Over the past 10 years, I've forged a warm, cordial, yet surface level relationship with my mom. We see each other a few times a year and mostly discuss work, health issues, my siblings, my children, our husbands, and how much money I'm making (or not!). I recently heard myself talking about this relationship and was ashamed to realize that I spoke from a place of blame: *She* is the superficial one, *she* is unaware and asleep, *she* is so self-involved.

My mother's friend Grace was a vibrant, jolly being whose exuberance and *joie de vivre* stood in stark contrast to my mother's emotional distance. Early memories of time spent with my mother are peppered with flashes of Grace: my brother and me posing for her camera on the back of her brand new VW "punch buggy" convertible, trips to the Canadian National Exhibition (known as "The Ex") with her in the late summer, and her squeal of joy when she babysat us and my stepfather called to tell us that we now had a baby sister. Grace married Rick around that time. He was tall and handsome, and reminded me of Burt Reynolds. Soon afterwards they had a baby girl of their own. Grace lived life large and was an alive, vibrant, and extremely capable woman. She was a role model for me—offering an alternative to the serious and studious approach to life I had chosen as a child of divorce.

Grace died of leukemia when her daughter was about two years old. I found it hard to believe that someone so powerful could succumb so fully to a disease. My mother told me the story of how Grace and her husband decided together when it was time to extinguish all of the life support systems. She wept as she recounted in detail Grace's last moments in which she said farewell to her friends, husband, and daughter. My sense was that as the mother of a little girl herself, the thought of having to consciously say goodbye to a child who was barely old enough to understand what was happening was unbearably painful for her. It was one of the few times that my mother dipped beneath the surface and allowed me to see her grief and sorrow.

Now, as I approach my 40th birthday, I find myself face to face with my own discomfort with intimacy: with myself and with other loved ones. A wall has been constructed which serves to keep me at a distance from *really* feeling certain emotions. At this point in my process of dismantling this wall, it appears the foundation is an enduring belief that I'm not good enough. It amazes me to uncover the roots which are so firmly planted and to observe the extent to which this belief and the wall hold me back from *my* full expression of my own joie de vivre!

Another memory floats up: A few years ago my friend's sister, Emma, died of cancer at the age of 30. I returned from the funeral grieving deeply and filled with sorrow, and felt a strong longing for my mom that was so unfamiliar to me. It had the energy of a lost and scared little girl who in complete despair cries, "I want my mommy." Mom was overseas, but somehow we managed to phone each other. I remember sobbing inconsolably as I related the story to her. She cried, too. A rare moment of connection made possible both by the many miles between us and a certain kind of sorrow that only a mother can feel.

As I lie here tonight, wondering why the story of Grace has suddenly downloaded itself into my mind, the word that is offered to me is Compassion. Compassion for my mother, for me, and for all of us.

The strategy of trying to separate myself from my emotions has been effective as a way of hiding my fear of being found to be inadequate, and my shame at surely not measuring up. And it's time to stop this. I feel an emerging easing of the harsh judgment I've heaped on the relationship I have with my mom. And an awareness that perhaps, at the core, we're not that different from each other after all.

*****************

The morning after writing this story, I awoke still mulling compassion and grace over in my mind, so I chose a Rune Card to see what wisdom it might offer. I received the card of *Kano* or Opening. Here's what it said:

> *This is the Rune of opening, renewed clarity, dispelling the darkness that has been shrouding some part of your life. You are free now to receive and to know the joy of non-attached giving.*
>
> *Opening is the Rune for the morning of activities for seriousness, clear intent and concentration, all of which are essential at the beginning of any endeavor. The protection offered by Kano is this: The more Light you have, the better you can see what is trivial and outmoded in your own conditioning.*
>
> *In relationships, there can now be a mutual opening up. You may be called to serve as the trigger, the timekeeper, through your awareness that the Light of understanding is once again available to you both.*
>
> *Recognize that while on the one hand you are limited and dependent, on the other you exist at the perfect centre where the harmonious and beneficent forces of the universe merge and radiate. You are that center.*
>
> *Simply put, if you have been operating in the dark, there is now enough light to see that the patient on the operating table is yourself.*[3]

I go into my day knowing that it's possible to cultivate the intimacy I so crave, yet am so afraid of. Grace has come full circle.

3 The Book of Rune Cards: Sacred Play for Self-Discovery, by Ralph Blum, October 1989, St. Martin's Press

# IT'S POSSIBLE THAT I'M THE ASSHOLE

I create my own reality.

I allowed my heart to soar
in your presence...back then
when we first met.

We turned to each other, clasped
hands and hearts and moved
into union, determined to succeed.

Then I saw something else...
something so wondrous it took
my breath away. I saw who
I could be.
I returned to you, excited to
share the news.

But you were not interested in
new things for us. You like things
the way they were before my discovery.
You asked me not to go,
stretching your hands towards me,
futile, as I danced away.

At first I blamed you -
you are not as advanced as me,
you don't get it,
you can't or won't meet me here.
Asshole!

Months deeper into the hurt it
occurs to me that
I create my own reality.
I have created this separation,
this pain.
It's possible that I am the asshole, after all.

What kind of mother leaves her children
or at best schleps them back and forth
between homes, just so she can be
"happy"?

What kind of woman leaves a man who
loves her as best he can, the only way he knows how,
in search of ecstatic connection and love?
Where there is a real possibility of ending up
alone and sad?

Only an asshole would do these things.
A selfish beast.
A passionate lover of life.

Like me.

# THE TRUTH AND THE WAY

Who am I?
Why am I here?

What is the thing that I'm called to offer now, that means the world to me?

I am a soul living in this temporary body.
I am a lover
I am mother to the children
We live in this beautiful, temporary home.

I am here to love, to be loved.
I am here to be guided and to guide.

What is calling me now?

Surrender deeply to love.
When I can remember that I am walking in partnership with Spirit and Earth, things are good.

# DON'T TURN AWAY

a steady diet
of terrible news hurts me
still, I keep looking

waiting for a way
to help, even just a bit
while the hot tears flow

perhaps this is it:
remaining present, awake?
it is not enough

one more thing to do
give love to every being
refusing hatred

this great love can spread
cover the entire planet
touching every soul

it is worth doing
no matter how small it seems
grace, affecting all

perhaps then we will
come home, together, again
One Great Human Family

# SURRENDER

My disinterest for things that used to taste good rises. Working myself to exhaustion, trying so hard to bring everyone on board, attempting to assuage the discomfort of beloved ones, the pursuit of fame and all the trappings that come along with it, being seen as the life of every party I attend, my need to be smart, entertaining, or deep. As my fatigue expands, I flip back to a journal entry from 18 months ago:

> *I think it's the striving that is losing its charge. It matters not anymore whether you see it my way. It is no longer my job to convince you that I'm right. If you've come with an intention to heckle me, to make me prove it, then you should really move on. Your insistence that I enter into battle with you only serves to take us all backwards, and I have no interest in that.*
>
> *What nourishes me now is the clean, clear swish of cool water in my mouth, the feeling of leaves crackling under my feet as I walk through the trees by the bluffs. Sitting with my teenaged son working on an algebra problem, with other moms while our kids practice basketball, playing cards or a board game as a family, just hanging out together. Catching up with friends. Moments of connection.*
>
> *I believe that we are all siblings in this Great Human Family. I want to walk, to dance, to live with those who can hold this view, too. Let's be happy together! What would be life-affirming now would be to join with those who understand what I'm saying and build something wonderful together.*

# TRANSFORMATION

## YESTERDAY

scattered woman
reacting to each problem
without direction

## TODAY

powerful presence
a creator of vision
led by desire

## TOMORROW

clear boundaries here
humble, not needing spotlights
joyous and complete

Yearning
to
Matter

# YEARNING TO MATTER

*Alongside the Wave of Insistence I shared about earlier in this book is a thread that runs through my life that I call "Yearning to Matter". I have felt so unseen, so unheard, so unimportant.*

*From the tumultuous environment in my younger years, where parents and grandparents would scream at each other while I watched my baby brother, through always feeling different at school (in an awful, never celebrated way), to having to push and drive and force my way in my work life, only to be discarded like a torn shirt after years of heartfelt service.*

*I suppose that is why I love working with human beings so much. It's my attempt to ensure they don't have to feel that way. Passionate about helping people who lead and influence many others to create a workplace where people know they matter, I've built the third chapter of my life around this.*

*These poems speak to the pain of feeling invisible despite wanting to offer great love, and the journey to being seen, heard, understood, and knowing that I matter.*

# UNJUST DESSERTS

*Please know that your own trauma may be triggered by this story.*

The sides of the white box refused to stay put after the tape was cut, but the lid still worked. I slid my finger in between to coax it open. Inside was the most delicious cake. Rich, dense, chocolate sponge oozing with the juice of that berry jam-like stuff they smeared between the layers, which alternated with thick chords of sweet-salty buttercream icing. Gigantic, whole strawberries perched atop fat clouds of whipped cream floating on top. The new bakery in our small Ontario town did not disappoint.

I already knew how yummy it was. We each indulged in a small piece that morning to celebrate my younger brother's 15th birthday, as was our family tradition. Harun's birthday was always extra special because he was born on Valentine's Day, the lucky duck. As soon as I cleared the dinner plates from the table, I took the box out of the fridge and set the cake on the counter. It would taste so much better when it came to room temperature.

Dad made his way down the stairs, the sound of his footsteps measured and even as always. A very senior leader at work, he was always proper, polite, and dignified. Like a king! Yet the stress of his recent separation from our stepmother was showing. A few more grey hairs amongst the dark curly locks, some extra padding around the tummy area, and it looked like his shoulders were slightly hunched forward now. He assured us their intention was to reconcile eventually; however, she and her 16-year old daughter had moved out for the time being. I couldn't have been happier.

"Make sure you keep some for me," Dad instructed as he headed out the side door, likely to visit *her*. "I'm going out for a while. Should be back by nine."

"I'm gonna watch my show," Harun announced as he tucked the broom and dustpan away and moved his skinny body through the door to the basement. His habit of heading to the basement immediately after meals hadn't been resolved by the departure of our stepmother. I took a few shallow, gentle breaths to ease away the sharp pain in my chest that always came when I thought of what she had done to him. Right after we moved here eight years ago, a newly blended family of five, she began to mistreat him. What kind of ruthless bitch sends a terrified little boy of seven to the basement by himself, night after night? If she didn't want him around, she could have at least let him watch the other TV in the family room on the main floor. Good riddance to her and her spoiled brat daughter. Even if Dad wanted to salvage things, I'd be happy to never see the two of them again.

A few minutes later, there was one sharp knock at the door. My heart leapt. My Valentine had made it after all. For the next couple of hours we would have the run of the house, just like a married couple. Maybe we could turn on the sauna later, or go sit on the fancy sofas in the living room, kissing tenderly then getting up to slow dance to "Careless Whisper" by Wham. That bitch never allowed us to enter the living room unless company came, and until recently, Dad only let me use the record player under his direct supervision. Everything was different now that she was gone. What fun we would have.

The smile on my face froze as I threw the door open and turned on the outside light. There was Dave, empty-handed, slouching against the wall with his thumbs hooked into his pockets, all smeary with dust, the stench of factory fumes wafting off of him. We had hooked up twice before, each time after running into each other at a local dance club, so this was a version of him I hadn't seen before. I looked up at him, surprised at how much taller his steel toed boots made him seem. Eight years my senior, he had a job for sure, but a factory worker? What a downer.

"Hey." He flipped back that long rocker-style hair that had initially attracted me. "I'm on a split from work. I only have an hour." He pushed past me into the foyer, dropping his coat over the rail. "I need a shower."

Dreams of a romantic Valentine's celebration fading, I convinced myself this was the next best thing. At least he made the time to come over, right? And, of course, I reasoned, he couldn't have gotten any flowers or chocolate for me since he had worked all afternoon. I should probably consider myself lucky that we were seeing each other tonight; we should make the best of it.

Back from the shower, he dropped the towel on my bedroom floor and shut the door.

"Come on. Take off your clothes. I'm in a hurry."

He nudged me further into the room until the edge of the bed caught the back of my knees, throwing me off balance. He shoved me down and climbed on top of me, pushing my shirt and bra up towards my neck.

I look up at his emotionless eyes.

"I can't. I have my period," I say, trying to use my firmest voice. My heart beats hard and fast.

"Who cares? A little blood doesn't matter."

His freshly shampooed strands of hair stung cold as the ends slapped my face. He wrestled my hands away and somehow unzipped my jeans.

"No," I whispered urgently, bucking my hips upwards in a futile attempt to get some space between us. He laughed. Got heavier. Kept going.

I didn't scream. All I could think of was Harun. *What will happen if he hears? If he comes in, he'll get hurt. He's so weak and scrawny; he's no match for Dave. Or maybe he'll tell Dad he heard me having sex. Dad will be so disappointed in me; I'm only 17 years old. I must stay quiet. I stop struggling. Better to just let it happen.*

My eyes traveled to that dark spot, high up there on the pink walls. *Dead spider? Missed corner when painting?*

Dave grunted, "Jesus, you're so tight."

No kisses. Thank God.

Dry hot pain. Like he had rubbed thick rough branches together to heat them up, then corkscrewed them deep inside me. *Never mind. It will be over soon. Dead spider, I conclude. I'll get it down later.*

* * *

"I need a clean shirt. What do you have?"

"Here."

I gave him my coveted soft green sweatshirt from our recent school play. I loved how it enveloped me in a soft, warm hug whenever I put it on, just like I imagined it would feel to be held by the loving boyfriend I had always yearned for.

"What the fuck is this?"

"It's the only thing I have that will fit you."

*Just hang in a few more minutes. He'll be gone.*

He spotted the cake on his way out. "That looks good. I'll have a piece before I go."

"Yeah, sure." I started to cut a narrow wedge.

"No, bigger. Good fucking makes me hungry."

He smiled and grabbed my bum, squeezing hard.

"Here." I handed him the plate, fantasizing how good it would feel right then to jam the fork deep into his narrow forehead.

Harun came upstairs. "Oh, hi."

"Hey, I'm Dave. This your birthday cake?"

"Yeah."

"Oh wow man, it's good."

He shoved another forkful between his thin lips.

I couldn't meet Harun's eyes. *Did he hear anything? Would he tell on me? What will Dad think of me if he finds out?* I busied myself putting stuff away, wiping off the counters. *Eat fast you greedy pig. Just finish and get out of my house.*

* * *

The shock began to wear off after Dad returned. I handed out plates of cake and we clustered at one end of the long table to eat. The quiet was deafening; silence being our new normal now that we were just three again. A burning heat rose through my cheeks as the throbbing of my heartbeat got louder and louder in my ears. Would Dad notice that something was wrong?

Later, I turned the shower on full force then gathered the entire curtain to one side and lifted it high up above the side of the tub. Moving the shower head in a wide circle I tried to wash as much of Dave out of my bathtub as possible. I climbed in. A wave of dizziness hit me, and a moment later I found myself on my hands and knees, gagging up that sinful cake and watching it go down the drain. The water streamed over my head as I sobbed, filling my ears and nose, muffling my cries. Too tired to scrub, I hoped the flow would take all traces of Dave off of my body.

But the shame was another matter; I sent it deep into myself, because I knew I was to blame. I invited him over. I didn't say, "No," when he said he wanted to shower. We'd had sex before, so he naturally expected more. I fell into a dreamless sleep, then got up and made my way to school. Nobody would ever know I was the shameful girl who got what she deserved, except me.

### *Author's Note*

*This is a work of creative nonfiction. The events are portrayed to the best of my memory. While the story is true, some names and identifying details have been changed to protect the privacy of the people involved.*

# THE PATH OF THE OTHER

Attempts, without malice
to rob you of the ability
to bring forward your gifts
will be made, perhaps many times

The position of their privilege
robs them of being able to see how it works

Illuminating this is risky
and often backfires

Angry *brown woman*, [insert your *otherness* here]
they will say,
who just played the race card
How dare she insult us like that?

And then, it becomes about them again

My wish is for another path
where they can put their indignation down
long enough to ask questions,
"How HAVE I contributed to her experience, consciously or not?
What can I learn if I open my eyes, ears and heart?"

Only then will my vision of our Great Human Family be possible.

# ENCHAINED

Speak up *graciously*
Speak your truth *gracefully*
Share your thoughts *carefully*
Be courageous *politely*
Write an article *but provide evidence*
Take a stand *but show us your credentials*
Take up space *but not too much*
Have an opinion *but don't be confrontational*
Be a leader *but let us go first*
Be fierce *but not too angry*
Don't be invisible *but let us be the experts*
Don't be quiet *just be careful*
Don't be loud *your passion is overwhelming us*
Your experience has validity *until our feelings get hurt*
You are welcome *as long as you don't ask us to change*

# ZERO SOME

Who gets to be big?
Who gets to be seen?
Who gets to be heard?

not me
it's not right
it's not fair

What to do?

Keep going, they say
keep following the intuition
the breadcrumbs
the light

Baby steps, they say

while they leap, crossing
galaxies with each step
gathering light and people
and never looking down once

they say:
It's not a zero sum game
little one!

so why does it feel
this way to me?

There there little one,
you just need to take the
next step, just the next
little step

One day you'll get here

for now
stay small
remain in the shadows
hidden from sight

Your turn will come

now let me get back to
my spotlight
I have important things to do
that you'll never be a part of

stay behind
remain below
you and your baby steps

I'll reach down to pat
your head comfortingly
if I happen to notice you, tugging
on my pant leg

but more likely I'll forget
we even had this years-long
interaction
cause I'm too busy with
all my stars

Who are you talking about?
That little one?

don't pay any attention
to her – she's insignificant
small, humble
we need
people like her to help
us see but we don't
need to see her, hold
her in the light or
really give her much regard at all

those people
were brought here
to serve us, not to be served
by us!

you could toss her a bone
every now and then
that will keep her quiet
and busy
gnawing on our scraps

# WILLING RAGE

Can you sit with my rage?

You say you want to help
heal this
You read books
You gather for polite
conversations with each other
A toe dipped into the pond
You feel better
You are doing something

But this journey demands
much more

You have the luxury of a reprieve
the remaining
one-hundred-and-sixty-six hours
per week

We do not
We are always on guard
remaining vigilant
twenty-four/seven/fifty-two
Always looking in
through the lens of *other*

Any relief is momentary
Peaceful moments
of comfortable co-existence are
fleeting, fragile, precarious
Lulled into thinking
we belong
we get yanked back
hard
the first time
we ask, inquire or point out
how you've missed us again
(I invite you to try
living like this
It is suffocating)

Can you be with this rage?

Find something solid
and hold on tight
This rage is a storm
brewing for centuries
so it may get a bit windy
Come prepared
to hunker down
We will be here for a while
Expect some damage

The monuments you built
to hold this up
need to be upended,
dismantled and hauled away
Things could get messy

No more neat
polite circling around
speaking cautious platitudes
and saying essentially
nothing

This rage is laden
with blood, tears,
anguish and impotence
that will make you
entirely uncomfortable
Please…don't defend now
If the tears and snot
start running
bring courage
and tissues
and just keep going

Have you touched the fire of your own rage?

I'm not talking about
the indignation
that arose three years
three months
or three weeks ago
when you proudly
became aware of
your own privilege
which, by the way
I've been keenly aware of
for about 50 years
Nor your newfound
authority in all things
D and I and E
Especially not
the saviour-oriented penance
that is important for you
to be seen to be making

I'm talking about
forging intimacy
with the
*exhausted*
*depleted*
*unhinged*
parts
yours and mine

Stand
in the fire
with us
Open your heart strings
feel in deep
You may lose
something
This is the cost
for human wholeness

Are you willing
to pay it?

# THE INVISIBLE WOMAN

she's your greatest fan
an advocate for your gifts
promoting your offer
and growing your community

selflessly
tirelessly
good heartedly
giving of her labour and love

*surely if I wholeheartedly jump in*
*to this that I have such passion for*
*I will receive a share in the return*
her misguided optimism says

funding her own development
flying beneath the radar
infinitely creative, always learning

Yet you don't won't or can't see her

The gaze flits over her in favour
of brighter façades, who know the rites:

The right words to say
The concepts to preach
The quotes of the learned ones

And settles for that
Easier
Less personally confronting
Pretty resonance of same

while she, eyes downcast,
filled with shame that doesn't belong to her
toils in the background

# Loving

# LOVING

*Another thread that you have no doubt picked up on as I've shared my story with you is the heartfelt commitment I have to service to others, care for the soul, and recognition of our shared humanity. Love has accompanied the pain of invisibility and the yearning to matter. Why not? Life is not about absolutes... all of this can be present at the same time.*

*These pieces are poems that speak to the many aspects of loving: love of children, crushes and infatuations, spousal love, endings of relationship, self-love, divine love, and more.*

# WHAT I WANT YOU TO KNOW

*My younger son and I were home together. Eating lunch, I inhaled a crumb of toast. After clearing it from my windpipe, I experienced a coughing fit leading to my throat swelling up inside. Suddenly, I couldn't breathe at all.*

*In that moment, a number of thoughts went through my mind:*

- *I can live without breathing for about one and a half minutes.*
- *Get help, FAST!*
- *I don't know how this is going to end.*
- *My son is keening in terror and there's nothing I can do about it. Even though this might be our last moment together, I can't worry about him right now.*
- *We need another adult here, NOW!*

*As I gasped my way into a 911 call, I went to the front door and opened it. The cooler air seemed to relax things and I was able to inhale a bit more air. By the time the firefighters and paramedics arrived I had almost fully recovered.*

*That was one of the most frightening experiences I've ever had. A few days later, as I reflected in my journal, I asked myself, if this was my last moment with my children, what would I want them to know?*

To my beloved children,

You are ENOUGH. You are good, you are lovable, you are important. No matter what you do, or don't do, you are enough just as you are.

I love you. I love you in the silly, snuggly, giggly times, I love you in the fierce, harsh, and angry times, I love you even when I'm sighing with frustration and in all the other times. I LOVE YOU!

You are not alone. Even when you think you're the only person who is experiencing something hard, joyful, painful, or challenging, I want you to know that others experience these things, too. The details will be unique to each person, but the essence is often the same. You are not the only one. Therefore, talk about your feelings, what it's like for you, how you see things. Connecting with others in this deeper way joins us and creates community and support.

You are human. It's okay to hold it together, AND it's okay to lose it! We all do both. It is normal and so are you. Nobody is perfect, including me, as you well know!

Life is precious. Each breath is a gift. Up until the choking incident, I used to think: *Life is short so there's an urgency to do what you're here to do, now.* I want to replace this with: *Life is beautiful so let's savour every breath, every moment while we're here. All of them: the good, the bad, the challenging, the wonderful.*

There is much to be grateful for. Pause often to take stock of all the people, resources, and structures in your life that support you. Thank them, out loud and often. Let them know how much their presence in your life means to you. This can be as simple as a friendly chat with the grocery store staff when you're there, or as easy as a short email to a friend or a phone call with a loved one.

Everything that happens is useful. This one can be really hard to take in, especially when bad things happen. *Out of the wound comes the gift.* I don't know who said that first, but it rings true for me every single time, even when what happens is excruciating.

Dance daily. Move your body every day in a way that feels good to you. If you like running, go for a run! If you don't like the gym, do something else! Moving feeds the body, mind, and soul in a way that no computer screen or television ever could.

Laugh daily. Or more than daily!

Do what needs to be done, AND make time for resting, daydreaming, and hanging out with yourself. Powerful insights can come from taking your attention away from the problem you've been focused on.

Partner with Spirit, with objective third parties, with others, and with yourself to create what matters most to you and the type of life you want to have. My circles of support are strong and robust, and continue to hold me as I navigate life.

Go outside. Play with friends. Do I need to say more about this one? I don't think so!

Thank you for the gift of your presence in my life.

Love, Mom

# INFATUATION

You proclaim this A Good Partnership.
Yet it feels selfishly luxurious to bring my selves to your spacious embrace.

You call me a healer; I want to claim that gift here.
Yet your wounds are withheld from me.

From time to time, I sense you slipping at the edge.
But you quickly right yourself, averting a fall.

I try to remain proper, sensible, cool.
Yet I am incapable of mastering the distant stance required
to pretend that this friendship has no impact on my soul.

What would happen if you revealed your wounds?
I imagine my hands on your heart…that tender place where fear is so heavily guarded. Allowing my light to flow into you, just as yours surrounds and holds me.

Silly girl you are dramatic, reckless, ridiculous, impulsive!
Stop searching for pain; making things more difficult than they need to be.
Just relax into the ease with which this friendship is unfolding.

Patience, steadfastness, restraint.
These are your gifts, not mine.

Sighing, I continue on my journey,
smiling as I feel your presence alongside.

# INFATUATION II

This moment is a gift from God.
A true blessing.
A reminder that love is possible and deserved.

Why do I always forget that a moment lasts only for a moment?

How I love and hate this illusion.
Sometimes it feels so real. I can *taste* the sweetness of its promise!
Then I emerge from the dream and find myself here, awaiting the
inevitable awakening.

*Dearest Beloved…you must remember to savour the moment then let it go.*
*This fleeting gift does not extend into the future. It was not ever meant to.*

I hang my head in shame at the grand fiction I mistakenly created.
Peace returns and life takes over
until the next time I am swept away by the passion
of undefended presence in our embrace.
When we bid each other farewell like the lovers we have been
and the spiral continues, despite my resolve to be better, stronger,
smarter this time.

Later, the hot tears of disappointment remind me
that a moment only lasts for a moment.
And this moment is a gift from God.

# AMBITIOUS HEALING

Inspired by Derek Wolcott's poem: *Love after Love*

I've been working hard for a better balance of energies within.
Validating the outcomes through comparisons, feedback and other external metrics.
Congratulating myself on the efforts I've made, thinking *this is what it means to heal.*

I even declared that I would now be *exquisitely tender* with myself.
How arrogant to think I could easily live into something so utterly foreign to my ambitious strategies!

In my yearning to be someplace I wasn't, I *acted as if* and made loud decisive resolutions to be *done with the old.*
Blinded by the illusion that I could simply snap my fingers and say goodbye forever to *that way.*

Just when I thought I had made it to the other side, the band snapped back and contracted me even further.
The intolerable emptiness moved into my core and whispered quietly to me:

*Harsh attempts to propel yourself to the next place won't work now.*
*Stop striving for change and start being it instead.*
*What's required is very different; in fact it is what you fear the most:*
*Only you can strengthen this container, then only you can fill it with love.*
*This is what it means to heal.*

# WHY?

Your fierce commitment
Kind heart, generous embrace
Openly loving

# A CHALLENGE TO LOVE

Don't come in here
Stop!
Entrance prohibited

Courageous defender…what evil do I represent?
How can I be so bad, such a threat, despite the love that is here?

Does the tree resist the wind?
Do the leaves shut out the sun?
Would the lake, given a choice, choose to repel the fish and birds and sunlight that glimmers so beautifully?

I think not.
I want to come in. Will you let me?
Knowing the blessings possible?

# HEALING RELATIONSHIP PRAYER

Divine Spirit,
please make me an instrument of peace
so that I will hold the space
for healing this relationship
and both of our hearts
remaining filled with myself,
the energy of the planet
and your Grace
maintaining my own healthy boundaries
while deeply connecting with another
remembering that there is nothing
to defend against.

# LET'S SAY

Let's say out loud
what our experience really is.

Let's sit here together by the fire
joining through the sharing and receiving of all life's learning.

Let's slow it down
so every voice has a chance to make its way in, through and around.

Let's remain soft enough to receive each other
willing to be molded with each addition of presence.

# ACCEPTANCE

And so it is time.
Time to let go, to say a final goodbye to you, to the dream, to what was real and what was not.
Time to accept us both in our imperfect perfection.
Time to allow the depths of my sadness to fill me as great sobbing hiccups arise and release through my belly, heart, throat, and eyes.

I sit in this excruciating and necessary in-between place with nothing to do but this: Turn and smile through wet lashes at what has brought me here.
Send blessings to it all and allow it to settle in my memory just as the soft snowflakes create a powdery blanket covering everything for a few moments before it becomes a part of the landscape by melting, being blown gently away, or getting moved to the side.

Tomorrow I will rise and make my way through the gateway to what beckons me next.

But for now I sit still, a cozy shawl over my quivering shoulders, feet planted in the Earth, gathering myself back together.

# DON'T FALL IN LOVE WITH YOUR THEORIES

Don't fall in love with your theories
for they will become a crutch
too heavily leaned upon
that threaten to crumble
when you happen upon a man, weeping
with the pain of his tender heart,
forcing you to act in destructive ways
if only to uphold the structure
long held, unquestioningly, as the truth

Don't fall in love with your models
that place one person higher than another
raising you up on a ladder, or worse,
a pedestal, that separates you
from the heart of human struggle
having you look down, with pity
and disdain on all those who
don't get it, can't get it, never had it
leading you to force teachings
on them that never included
them in the first place
leaving them perpetually oppressed
under the guise of benevolence

Fall in love with your own heart
with the seed of radiance deep inside
that knows who you are, where you
came from and how you are part of
the sisterhood of humanity
and guides you into a quiet place
of sitting, ripening and
remembering so you can be broken open
by teachings and truths of those
who don't and won't be shaped to fit your mold any longer
whom you previously and compulsively and
mistakenly tried to save,
opening yourself instead to infinitely greater
possibilities in this dance of mystery and
wonder, we call life

Sacred
Exchanges

# SACRED EXCHANGES

*The sacred is the ultimate unconditionally loving parent. It will welcome you back every time you choose to return to it. Yet it is so easy to ignore what is sacred in favour of tending to the daily tasks, requests, and needs that I feel obliged to meet. Almost like there's an unspoken value equation at play: If I just work harder it will all be finished, and THEN I can go outside, walk to the bluffs, relax with a beloved one or listen to beautiful music and dance around my kitchen.*

*Then come the moments when I set all of that aside and give myself the gift of a walk, or a quiet hour with a candle and my music. I'm amazed at how much ease this offers me. Inspiration arrives. Guidance and clarity come. Connections are made in a few minutes that I previously worried over for weeks.*

*Most of the poems in this book arrived when I wasn't "working hard". The words cascade from sacred sources: Mother Earth, a tree, a body of water, the witnessing of humanity in process, straight through me and out through my pen into my journal.*

# OUR HUMAN FAMILY

It was an early morning flight, two days after a big snowstorm, and the security lines were packed full of people.

We were a collection of individuals all focused on getting through the drudgery of the airport process: take off shoes, laptops out of bags, any liquids? I tried to remain positive, but I have to admit that my default has been to regard the security folks connected to the process they represent as pains in the behind.

This particular morning there was a gentleman just ahead in the line who was holding things up. He had placed his items on the table but now wasn't moving forward. This caught my attention, and as I gazed at him I noticed he was trembling. I began to wonder if he was okay, and was just considering moving in towards him to ask when he staggered backwards with two large steps, then fell, hard, striking his head on the table of the adjacent lane as he went down.

There was a sharp, collective intake of breath in a moment of nothingness as we all took this in. He lay on the ground, a small puddle of blood beginning to form under his head. I was certain he was dead. Then the whole picture came alive. Someone yelled, "Call 911!" A woman standing behind me moved towards him. Security personnel jumped over their various tables and conveyors to assist. I observed it all, my hand over my mouth to muffle my silent scream of utter despair. Then a wave of relief moved through the room as we saw his eyes fluttering and his body moving ever so slightly.

While it would be easy to make this story about me and how I berated myself in those moments just after it happened for not moving towards him quickly enough, what I really want to tell you is what I noticed afterwards.

We became a family. Our "game faces" that we put on when we entered the airport that morning (or perhaps when we left our homes?) were no longer necessary. Those of us who were not directly involved in caring for him continued through the process, but the emotional field was different now. We were more connected, we began speaking to each other; people became more REAL.

I turned back to watch his rescue unfold and heard a security guard asking a different gentleman if he was okay. He had witnessed the incident too, and looked pale and a bit shaken. She reached out and placed her hand on top of his and as she patted it said, "I know, I know." This moment of tenderness is seared upon my heart and has left me forever changed.

That morning an upsetting accident served to remind a handful of us that we are not separate from each other. We may occupy a role in any given moment: security, passenger, official, elderly, young, etc. But these are just roles. They are not our identities! What was so beautiful about this shocking incident was that it helped us drop these roles for a moment so we could stand together as humans.

As I sat at my departure gate sipping my tea, someone beside me was talking about the incident. I turned to this stranger, my brother in our human family, and asked if he knew how the story had unfolded. He smiled and said that the paramedics arrived, cared for the gentleman, and eventually had him standing up and talking. My heart filled with gratitude for this happy ending.

# ENTER THE SACRED

*This poem came through as I walked through the grounds of the University of Toronto in October 2017 – a special place in my hometown. As I marveled at this carved-out piece of tranquility in the middle of a bustling city, I felt ashamed. How could I have forgotten about this place that illuminates illusion, lightens my load, and soothes my soul? These words are the reply I heard:*

Come into the garden
And put your burden down.
We have made this place for you
With a canopy of majestic trees, a symphony of birdsong
and the peacefulness of your sentient siblings
So that you can remember who you are, who you've always been
and that you never walked alone.

Come, rest now.
Let the gentle breeze caress your soul as
the sun recharges your spirit and
the earth renews your foundation.

Have you forgotten that we are here?
That happens from time to time.
No matter.
Just hear our whisper in the leaves:

*You can always return*
*No need for forgiveness*
*This is your home*

# JOY ENDURES

Even though we're in this cloudy mess
the sun still shines

Even though we can't touch each other
we can still connect

Even though the playdates ceased,
little Ava is excited for her first day at school

Even though the morning air brings a chill
I can still enjoy my coffee outside

Even when what we thought we knew proves wrong
the human spirit is infused with the Divine

Even if you've lost your way
there is still hope of being found

Even when what we've built burns down
birds still call out to each other

I don't know what will happen next
and maybe I never did anyway

# ANOTHER BEGINNING

Warm sunlight on my face
is soothing after so many days
of denying my true nature

*Darling, come and sit*
it seems to say
*I will envelop you*
*in my healing embrace and all*
*shame and*
*anger and*
*disappointment will fall away*

A soft breeze comes in long languid waves
gently dusting the dis-ease from my field.
Earth feels firm yet spongy
under my feet clad in the slightest of slippers
so that I may make contact
with this Great Mother

Cicadas and crickets and birds
sing their symphony together as if
conducted by some universal ringmaster
who knows exactly how to match
the rhythm of my emotions

Silence
then just crickets
then a rising cicada buzz
climbing to a dazzling crescendo
then fading back to
a quiet hum

The sweet chirps of the
birds punctuating the pauses
with their happy assurance:

*It's ok.*
*Nothing bad will happen*
*as you nourish yourself.*
*There's no punishment in store*
*because you spent 20 minutes here.*
*There are only rewards:*
*flow, calm, clarity, peace.*

The waterfall becomes primary
reminding me that
flow comes from
honouring my true nature

I smile to myself
as I prepare to walk on.
Grateful to begin again.

# MUSIC GOT DROPPED

*It is in the silent moments that the truth can be heard. This poem came through when I was on a long airplane ride from Toronto to Denver. I was going to gather with some beloved colleagues after a busy time of serving in all arenas of my life.*

Silence underpins the cacophony of voices shouting, "Me! Me! What about me?"

Suddenly I stop running and notice what is no longer present.

Music got dropped.

By this I don't only mean the beautiful music I once enjoyed listening to, although it's absolutely part of what is absent.

I mean the beauty and richness of the colourful tapestries that used to wrap around and between things.

Those elements that enlivened us, invited us to dance joyously, to waste time in the explorations of the tangents.

Beautiful music seems so much less valued in favour of WORK and RESULTS and EVIDENCE and PROVING.

The loss squeezes my heart as I take this in…music got dropped!

Like that succulent mango that got forgotten in the back of the fridge and you find it one day drained of its life force, flesh dry and skin wrinkled.

Don't punish yourself if you too have dropped the music. It happens in an instant.

Will you pick music up, welcome it back, cradle it in your arms, smile lovingly at it, and weep your apologies as you stroke its beautiful face, run your fingers through its hair, and take in that uplifting scent?

I will.

I bow my head toward the heart of music then begin painting long swirls and wiggly lines all over these stark walls that mysteriously constructed themselves around my own.

I don't know what comes next.
Ridicule?
Loss?
It matters not.
Whatever may pass will make itself known soon enough.

# WEARY WARRIOR

The weary warrior stands
Magnificent limbs draped downwards
Holding space for all

His arms warmly open
to encircle me with love
*I am here for you,* he whispers,
*come, relax, rest, restore in my embrace.*

He is infinite love.
And so am I.

# WHAT WOULD THE EARTH SAY, IF SHE COULD SPEAK THROUGH ME?

surrender, surrender Dear One
relax into the arms of the Mother
and know that you are home

put down your weapons
let down your hair
set it all down
it doesn't serve you now

turn towards yourself

turn towards each other

let love flow
bow, smile, let tender
warm-heartedness flow
across the breathways of the sky and sun and
wind and breeze

allow yourself to be enlivened
from the inside out now

let love flow
you are sisters and brothers in
One Great Human Family

can you see it?
can you feel it now?

this great pause that you are
invited to take
will nourish what is here
what has always been true

soak up this opportunity
revel in this pause
let the goodness of your true nature
prevail

send gratitude, appreciation
and joyful wishes across the
oceans
soon, the new way will emerge
you'll know it when it comes through

until then, rest

allow the sun to soak into your cells
let the breeze caress your skin
feel the threads that
connect you to each other

smile kindly upon each other
you are home

# DO IT NOW

Now. Now. Do it now Dear One.
The fire you fear is nothing compared to the risk of dying in silence.
This is your gift that you were put here to use.
Go Now Serve
The world is waiting…yearning for…craving your message, your great love, your compassion.
Nobody else can serve in exactly this way.
You fear your message is redundant…NOT TRUE!

Go Now NOW

Let your voice be a testament to what you have cultivated, what you know is true, what is so crucial.
Please Dear One, speak now!

As you allow your great love to wash over the world you can also open yourself to receive love.
You think you're powerful now? Ha! Just wait.
You have no idea the impact you will have when you become a circuit with this love. Cycling it out and then allowing it in.

Go NOW.
We sit here with arms outstretched, palms open, just waiting.
We are so thirsty for your love.

You are not crazy.
There is nothing to defend against.
Go now. Come home to the Divine purpose you were made for.

Go forward with ease, joy but also the urgency that you feel…it is not unwarranted.

You are held
You are loved
You are enough
You are AWESOME
There is always enough
Nothing to fear, no need to fret
It is enough

Now Go.

# MANTRA FOR DIFFICULT DAYS

I am held
I am loved
I am enough

There is peace
There is love
There is enough

# RETURN TO DANCE

Return to dance and let the gentle
undulation of your deepest waters
begin to loosen the truth you are
guarding so tightly.

The world needs your voice, your truth
and your purpose!

Dance and your truth will be set free.
Chant away the defenses and surrender
sing, draw, write and paint your purpose into being.

Oh beautiful One!
This is your time.
We welcome you with open hearts.

Let the embrace of
your soul stir your actions
and may your deepest gifts come forth
to heal every member
of our Great Human Family.

# ENOUGH'S INVITATION

never done
always seeking
keep going

it's exhausting

the myth of busy
badge of honour
so enticing!

offers redemption

what if
you were enough
simply because you exist?

ponder that for a moment

feel the ground
breathe the air
allow yourself to

be found

# THE DAWN OF THE FIERCE LOVE

**(formerly named For The Shy Ones and Earth Poem)**

Surrender, surrender Dear One
Allow me to hold you
Revel in the beauty of The Mother.
All that you seek is here for you!
No more need for striving
There is nothing to push forward
Take leave of your fears now
You are home.

Dear One,
follow only this: the joy, the sweetness, the love, the passion
Dance with utter abandon and sensual wildness
Why not?
Why not?
Your shyness does not serve the world

This is the dawn of the fierce love!
Gather your tribe and dance with furious passion.
This is what we need now;
you are the Ones we have waited for.
It is time to come home.

# UNITY

May there be peace

May there be love

May there be connection
so strong that it
holds across oceans and lands

May we revel in the beauty of
our radiance

Living lives of purpose & meaning

Experiencing joy and prosperity

A network of light that
encircles the planet
holding each and every One

We belong
because we exist

# MY INVITATION TO YOU

Beloved readers, I now hand this all over to you. I've taken the risk to step out of the safety of invisibility by sharing what is so present in my heart, body, and soul with you. It's your turn now.

Are you willing to look more closely inside? To work with the rich heart matter of your own life and all of your experiences—joyful and shattered, smooth and bumpy, empowering and traumatic? To come home to yourself?

I am certain that you can reconnect to the deeper truth, innate knowing, and heart's longing that lies deep within. Maybe you've been trained to totally discount your wise inner teacher, your intuition, and the guidance that lies in sources above, below, and all around you. Most of us have learned that logic is king, trusting only what is provable, believing it only if it can be quantified. So the road ahead to come to love and trust yourself will be challenging.

And I know you can do it.

What emerges on the other side of this exploration are infinite possibilities for new ways—I call them "third ways"—of living, loving, and working that go beyond black and white, right and wrong, good and bad. Polarities dissolve and separation ceases. People come together and create paths forward that bring joy, prosperity, and justice to all.

This is the dawn of the fierce love! It is time to come home.

Love and hugs,

Shahmeen

P.S. Come and join me for deeper explorations of your truth, your life and your leadership!

You can find my corporate leadership development offerings at: anjalileadership.com and we are always up to interesting things at: thishumanbeing.com.

I can't wait to get to know you!

# ACKNOWLEDGEMENTS

This book would not have been written, let alone published, without the support of my guides, teachers, colleagues, and clients.

To Deborah Ager, my book midwife, who patiently helped me find and land on a structure to hold all of these poems and pieces together meaningfully, you rock! Your beautiful gift of listening and hearing, then creating magic sentences out of my ramblings continues to amaze me and I am so grateful for your love and care.

To Laura Di Franco, the fiercest badass healer and publisher who guided the transformation of this manuscript into form, I bow to you. From our first conversation I knew I'd been seen and our second conversation showed me what excellent competent hands I am in. Thank you for holding me in the fire when it would be all too easy to back away and hide in the shadows.

To Heidi Walk, who first saw the seed of radiance in me and more importantly TOLD ME what she saw, I am forever grateful! I will never forget how you called me forth to walk the path that my heart yearned for instead of the one I was always told I was supposed to want. Do you know what a gift you are to me?

To Sue Griggs, Mary Murphy, Helen House, Suzanne Scurlock-Durana, Marina Toledo, Shavasti, Deborah McCrea, and Adrianne Sequeira; all amazing coaches, teachers, and therapists who patiently held/hold space for my endless spirals through healing my not enoughness. I thank you from the bottom of my heart.

To Ranjini George, my beautiful meditation and writing teacher who has held space, called me forth, supported me, and loved me into becoming the writer I am today, I feel so lucky to have found you. Thank you for your support, your feedback and most of all for showing me what equanimity and self-love looks like in real life.

To Heather Graham, Kat Hay, Carolyn Tilden, and Kathryn Snyder, my beautiful, powerful sisters in the journey, I bow to you. Your willingness to be real and raw, to dive deeply into the work and our relationships, to have the most difficult conversations with love, authenticity, and care has helped me become the person I am today. Not to mention what profound effect we've had with our clients through our partnerships. I love you all so much!

To Dan Holden, solid mentor and fierce ally as I jumped through hoops, clawed my way up walls, and broke ceilings into an eleven year chapter of such richness in the The Leadership Circle™ universe, your partnership has meant the world to me. That we still continue to work our mischief together is one of the great joys of my life.

To Jim Anderson, my beloved friend, I continue to be awed by your boundless generosity of time, interest, and spirit and your magical ability to stretch time to include it all. You hold me in my magnificence like no one else and I am so so so grateful for your presence in my life.

Thank you to all of my colleagues. Barbara Emmanuel, Chris Wahl, Barbara Braham, Paula Bourne, Melanie Parish, Mel Dowdy, David Womeldorff, and Bob Anderson, your work and our work together has helped to build this solid foundation under my feet that I stand on as I continue to evolve my gifts and expand my offerings.

Thank you to my clients for placing your trust in me and for being willing to dive deeply into the integration of exquisite self-awareness and extraordinary leadership. Special love goes out to the members of the Power Pause and The Well, the two communities that grew out of the disruption of 2020 and continue to evolve. You have proven my hypothesis true: that the greatest gift you could ever give another is the gift of your loving presence. I watch you give and receive that together every day and nothing could make me happier!

To Team Anjali: Jenny Haase, Kathryn Snyder, Karen Abrams Gerber, Dan Holden, and Joanna Cotton, thank you for saying YES to the adventure! I can't wait to see where the next years take us. I feel so blessed to be in this experiment with you.

These poems were written over the past 20 years and reflect on my entire life experience to date. A project like this does not happen without the support and encouragement of family.

To my parents, thank you for choosing to make Canada your home way back in the 1960's. Because of that choice, my brother and I were born in the most awesome country on the planet! I am grateful for this every day.

To Peter, my step-father, thank you for your solid, enduring, and everlasting support of me and my family. I'll always remember how you taught me to "give a little nod to the gods" as you spilled a little olive oil off the edge of the pan while cooking. This was my first introduction to the existence of beings beyond the tangible world.

To Linda, my Spirit Mother, whom you heard from in the beginning of this book, thank you for being the gift of light, love, and unconditional support that you are in my life. You have stayed close throughout my awakening and development for more than 30 years...do you know how amazing that is? I love you so much!

To my siblings and your families...thank you for your care, support, and interest in this book and the journey it took to get here. I love you all.

To the father of my boys, thank you for creating these beautiful children with me and for being willing to conclude our marriage with dignity and grace, while continuing to co-hold a container of love and support with me for the sake of the well-being of the boys.

To Juan, my partner in life and in purpose, I love you! Your generous heart and deeply caring spirit mean the world to me. Thank you for stepping into your calling. You are a gift to your clients. Thank you also for bringing Sara into my life. She is an angel.

And finally, to Jordan and Lukas, my children. Thank you for always reminding me that I am enough. Yes, I am crying while I write this. I am so proud of the young men that you both have become. You are resilient, independent, and loving souls. What more could a mother hope for? My love for you stretches as far as the entire circumference of the Earth, times a million.

# ABOUT THE AUTHOR

Shahmeen Sadiq, Master Certified Coach, founded Anjali Leadership Inc. in 2005, and has guided the development of leaders from a wide variety of industries including insurance, government, consulting, healthcare, education, banking, hospitality, and faith organizations. Since 2013, she has served as adjunct Leadership Faculty at the University of Notre Dame, and was the first female faculty member of The Leadership Circle, where she certified and mentored about a thousand coaches over her tenure from 2008-2019.

Shahmeen creates spaces where people feel that they belong, and she teaches and guides her clients to do so, as well. In 2009, she was honored by the International Coach Federation with a Prism Award for one such project: large system healing and culture change within a fractured not-for-profit organization.

These days she is focused on facilitating essential, intimate, and difficult explorations with committed, courageous, and resilient senior leaders of